HARRY KANE
The Hurricane

A special thank you to Yonatan Ginsberg, Yaron and Guy Ginsberg.

Cover photos © front: Reuters – Carlos Barria
                        Back: Reuters – Dylan Martinez

Cover design: A. Pikarski

Inside page layout: Lazar Kackarovski

Library of Congress Cataloging-in-Publication data available.

ISBN: 978-1-938591-58-7

eBook ISBN: 978-1-938591-61-7

Published by Sole Books, Beverly Hills, California.

www.solebooks.com

Harry Kane The Hurricane

Michael Part

Sole
BOOKS

To Ros & Laurie & David & Sarah
Who introduced me to the beautiful game

CHAPTER 1

TO TOTTENHAM & BEYOND

Charlie Kane charged through the Chingford house in Essex, breathless. When he got to Harry's room, he burst in and raced across to the bed, scattering soccer balls and orphaned socks, and shook his 11-year-old brother awake.

"T-they want you down at the training center!" he said, finally taking a breath.

"Let me sleep," Harry mumbled, groggy. "There's no training today!" He opened one eye for a look, groaned, then rolled over and tried to get back to sleep.

Charlie yelled. "Tottenham!"

The room grew silent.

Outside, a robin chirped.

At that moment, Harry sat bolt upright in shock.

"Wait, what-?!"

Charlie grinned. "Well, at least your head didn't spin around."

"Dad got the news," he said.

Minutes later, Harry rushed to his dad and mom, who were having breakfast.

"Good morning," his dad Pat smiled and exchanged a proud look with his mom Kim.

"Morning. Is Charlie pulling my leg?" Harry asked.

"You didn't wash your face," his mom pointed out.

"In a minute," Harry said, still breathless.

"I got a call from a scout," Pat said. "Mark O'Toole. Been watching you for quite a while."

"Really?" Harry was the skeptical son.

"No joke, Harry," Pat said, looking real serious. "Tottenham wants you at their development center for a trial!"

Everyone's eyes fell on Harry.

Harry took a breath and closed his eyes for a moment. A grin spread across his face. He opened his eyes and began chanting. "ONE OF US! ONE OF US! HARRY KANE IS ONE OF US!" He danced around.

Everyone laughed.

"This is the happiest day of my life!" Harry shouted.

The Tottenham Hotspur training center at Spurs Lodge in Epping Forest was just off the M11 in Chigwell, about 5 miles away. Harry rolled down his window as they drove up to the blue and white gate with the big white sign announcing *SPURS LODGE*. A security guard trotted out of his box. "Yes, sir?"

"Harry Kane has come for his trial," Pat announced sticking his chest out.

The guard checked his clipboard and grinned. "Very good, sir," he said politely and opened the gate for them.

"Grandpa Eric would be so proud!" Harry said from the backseat. Pat gunned the engine and drove the car onto the grounds.

"To be sure he would," Pat said. "You didn't get your talent from *my* side of the family."

"He loved the Spurs!" Harry chimed in.

"Almost as much as we do," Pat mused.

Pat parked the car. "All right then, son. Get in there and show them what you got," he said.

Harry opened the door. "Aren't you going to watch?"

"I'll watch from in here," Pat replied. "It's freezing."

Harry laughed and walked around to his father's door. He wore his favorite white Tottenham shirt. "*I'm* not cold."

"That so? Then why are you shivering?"

"I'm just scared."

"What of?"

"Missing my chance."

Pat opened his car door, got out, and hugged his son. "You put your lucky shirt on, right?"

"Yeah."

"And did anything change since the last time you were brilliant out there on the pitch?"

"No."

"Then, son, you have a hundred percent chance of hitting the bull's-eye."

Harry looked up at his dad. "Thanks, Dad."

"And another thing."

"What?"

Pat winked. "Have fun."

Harry flashed a smile and gave his father a thumbs up, then ran through the gate and out onto the field, passing the sign stating boldly: *U13 Trials*. He took his place at the end of a line of about two dozen boys, most of them older than him. He didn't care about the age or the height. He was used to being the smallest guy out there.

John Moncur, the head of the Spurs Youth, split the boys into two teams.

At Ridgeway Rovers, then Arsenal, then Watford, Harry had played in goal and midfield, but eventually they always moved him forward, where he delivered the goods with loads of goals. That was what he loved most. That was what he did best. Spanking the ball to the back of the net.

Moncur pointed at Harry.

"Harry, you play up front!" Moncur said.

Harry stared at him for a moment, dumbfounded. Was Mr. Moncur a mind reader?

In the parking lot, Pat moved forward for a better view. He knew what was coming.

Five minutes into the training match, George Moncur, John's grandson, passed the ball to Alex Pritchard, who had just come racing down the line. Alex passed to Harry who made a run into the box and with a quick move, passed a defender, and chipped the ball over the goalie's head into the right corner of the net.

Harry made it look as easy as his hero – Spurs star striker, Teddy Sheringham.

Harry put his arms in the air and bounced excitedly up and down on a springy plot of grass as his teammates surrounded him, congratulating him.

"Nice one, Harry!" John Moncur shouted.

Pat, back in the parking lot, raised his arms and bounced excitedly up and down just like his son out on the field. He was proud of his boy.

Harry and the guys he trained with had six weeks to prove themselves. Only a few would make it and Harry had his doubts.

When the six weeks were up, by the end of summer, Harry, George, and Alex walked off the field at Spurs Lodge.

"You're so brilliant at passing, George, and Alex, I wish I could dribble like you," Harry said as they walked toward their families in the car park.

"Leave it to Harry to big up everyone else," Alex said. "You were sick!"

"Nah," Harry said. "When I was at Ridgeway, they told me I was the best player on the squad, same at Watford. But here – I'm just average."

George shook his head. "What are you talking about? My grandpa loves you. You are a brilliant striker!"

"Too right," Alex said to him. "What are you worried about?"

"The letter," Harry said. He was talking about the season retaining letter a boy got, *if* he was invited back. For Harry, it meant moving up to his U14 team.

"You're kidding!" George laughed. "You're worried you're not coming back?"

Harry blushed. "I'm always worried."

"And always annoying."

They all shared a laugh.

Harry spotted his father's car with his father leaning against the front fender, arms folded across his chest, waiting. Grinning. Harry turned to George. "Well, I guess I'll see you next year."

"Yep," George said. He watched George and Alex as they went on their way and took a deep breath trying his best to switch off that sinking, worried feeling.

A couple days later, the letter arrived. Harry watched the mailman shove all the letters and magazines through the mail slot and move on to the next house. He dived onto the pile, mostly junk, shuffled through in a thunder of anxiety, finally finding the letter addressed to him from Tottenham Youth with John Moncur, in bold script, below the logo. He pressed the letter to his chest and closed his eyes. And prayed.

Pat and Kim and Charlie were waiting for him when he came into the kitchen, clutching the unopened letter from Spurs Lodge. "Is that your letter?" Kim asked.

"Yeah," Harry stammered.

"Well, open it, stupid!" Charlie quipped.

"You do it, Dad," Harry said and handed it to his father, his hand visibly shaking.

Pat shook his head. "Since when are you such a coward?" He tore open the envelope, unfolded the letter, and read it.

And frowned.

No one said a word.

"What's the matter?" Harry asked, his heart sinking.

"It's a release," Pat mumbled, looking up into his son's eyes. "They don't want you back."

Harry didn't know what to do.

Except run.

Seconds later, the front door of the Kane home burst open and Harry charged out and kept running up the road until he reached the nearby park. He leaned against a tree to catch his breath and looked up when he heard the noise of boys playing.

A short distance away, some boys played soccer in an open expanse. He wiped his tears and watched. It was a five-a-side pick-up and it brought the memories flooding back. As the boys played, Harry could almost hear the roar of 26,359 fans cheering, echoing off the stadium seats in White Hart Lane. It reminded him of his first Spurs match, when he was an over-energetic four-year-old, sitting with his family in the good seats; a family who loved soccer more than anything.

CHAPTER 2
THE RELEGATION ZONE

1997 was the second warmest August on record in London, and on Sunday the 10th, Harry went to his first match at White Hart Lane. The Spurs against Manchester United.

Harry, just four years old, heard the crowd even with the car windows rolled up. Even over the rattling sounds of the engine, as they waited in line to pull into the parking lot. The stands were already filling up. The roar of the Spurs supporters coming from inside the stadium beat against the car windows like a bass line and it made Harry's heart race. He looked over at his older brother, Charlie, sitting next to him in the backseat. Charlie had done this many times before, gone to matches at the Lane, and he knew what to expect.

"We're gonna win today, right, Charlie?" Harry asked.

"Yes," Charlie replied without opening his eyes. He looked like an older version of Harry, only huskier.

"If you want us to win, you have to show your support," his mom said.

"We're 20th," his dad quipped. "Fat chance of us beating Man U, if you ask me."

"Man U are in first," Kim explained. "All *our* good players are playing for *them*."

"Like who?" Harry asked.

"Teddy Sheringham for starters," Charlie said, "And David Beckham."

"His grandad is a season ticket holder here. Diehard Spurs fan, just like us," Pat said. "Becks trained in the Spurs academy."

"I miss Sheringham," Kim said.

"Life *was* better when Sheringham played for the Spurs," Pat sighed.

He parked the car and they all got out and walked into the stadium.

Pat and Kim found their seats and sat next to each other, putting Charlie and Harry on Pat's side. The seats were on the 50-yard line, halfway up. You couldn't get any better seats and Pat and Kim had planned this outing since before the start of the season. It was a promise to their youngest son.

Pat immediately picked up the conversation where they left off. "You know why we're down to 20, don't you?" He didn't wait for an answer. "I'll tell you why. Because Gerry's still your man there, that's why." He was talking about the Spurs' manager, Gerry Francis. He didn't like him much so he was emotional and spit his words out.

"What happened to us, Dad?" Charlie asked. "We've got David Ginola and Les Ferdinand, they should help. What's happened to our Spurs?"

"Relegation, that's what," his dad spat.

"I'm thirsty," Harry said.

Pat gave his youngest son a look. "Okay, not too many fizzy drinks, I don't want to be taking you to the bathroom and missing the match, you hear?"

"OK, Dad," Harry and Charlie said in unison.

Kim turned to Pat. "That goes for you too."

"Yes, dear," Pat said and lovingly took her hand.

The moment was interrupted by the roar of the crowd as the squads trotted out on the field and the game started.

Harry was so excited he could hardly breathe. He sat glued to his seat the entire first half. Despite what Harry thought was great playing, not much happened in the first 65 minutes. Then Paul Scholes was subbed by David Beckham and Harry was on his feet, cheering madly.

Pat looked up at his son and pulled him back in his seat. "Take it easy, son, he's on the other team."

His father was right. Despite the family love for the Spurs, Harry was more thrilled by Sheringham and now Becks, than his own team. He blushed. "Sorry, Dad," he muttered then returned his attention to Beckham on the field. He kept his mouth shut because he worried if he liked Man U too much, they might not take him to any more games.

In the 82nd minute, Nicky Butt scored for Man U. A minute later, Spurs center-back Ramon Vega added an own goal to the tally.

Pat, Kim, and Charlie were devastated as they walked back to the car, but Harry felt like he was walking on a cloud. He'd loved every minute of the match.

"Dad?"

"Mmm?" Pat responded, still scowling and hurting from the Spurs' loss.

Harry grinned. "Someday, I'm going to play for the Spurs," he said.

"Course you will, son," Pat replied with a smile.

"What about England?" Charlie asked with a smirk.

"England too!" Harry said. "At the World Cup!"

Pat draped his arm over Harry's shoulders. "It'll happen. All you have to do is never give up."

"I won't," Harry said.

And as it turned out, Harry never did.

CHAPTER 3

CHINGFORD & THE RIDGEWAY ROVERS

Charlie appeared in the doorway from the kitchen, barefoot, legs spread ready to block. Harry raced down the hall from the other direction, straight toward his big brother, dribbling a wad of rolled-up socks. When he was almost on top of him, he nutmegged the wad through Charlie's legs, shouldered past, banging into both walls, and disappeared out the doorway to the kitchen.

Kim stood in the middle of the kitchen, incredulous, as her son came sailing in. "Take it outside!" she shouted.

"Sorry, Mom!" Harry replied, skidding to a stop, picking up the ball of rolled-up socks, sitting down at the kitchen table. "It won't happen again."

"Oh really? You mean you'll actually listen to me? Since when?"

Harry blushed and shrugged. He knew she was right about listening. It was just that it was hard stopping a game. Even with a wad of smelly socks.

"He'll listen to you now that the Ridgeway tryouts are coming," Charlie said, sitting down next to his younger brother and ruffling his hair. They all shared a laugh.

Kim plunked down a bowl of cereal in front of each of them and one at an empty seat. "We moved here so you boys could have a bigger backyard to play in, so what do you do? You play in the house."

"Harry wants to play for the Spurs," Charlie said.

"I want to make them champions," Harry added.

Pat stopped eating and eyeballed his youngest son. "Excellent idea. But *you* don't decide to play for a club like the Spurs; *they* do. So, while you're waiting, how about we start with Ridgeway and work our way up?"

"You don't think he's too young?" Kim asked.

"He's six! Old enough to go to work!" Pat joked. "To be sure, he's small for his age, but he has it in him. He's glued to the ball every spare minute. The street…the park…the field…"

"…the house," Kim said, finishing his sentence.

"Exactly! And he's good," Pat said.

Harry blushed. He always got embarrassed when someone praised him.

"I want to!" he chimed in.

Pat leaned over the table and looked at his son in fake seriousness. "Then I think we'd better get you into a proper club before you break everything in the house!" he said and laughed when he saw Harry's face turn red.

"Line up over here, boys!" Dave Bricknell shouted. The coach and co-manager of the team was bundled-up in a blue-and-white Ridgeway wind-breaker with a warm gray sweater underneath. He was surrounded by a group of boys all eager to play.

Harry stood near some benches and took in the field, the coach, and the kids. They were all taller than him and they all looked too old to try out for the U7 team.

The hot summer had rapidly moved to a bone-chilling fall. The Ridgeway Rovers tryouts were held at the Loughton Rugby Club on Squirrel's Lane in Buckhurst Hill in Essex. It was where the team played their mini ball. The club was less than a mile from the Peter May Sports Centre in nearby Chingford, which was home base for the Rovers. The big boys.

Dave Bricknell, the coach, ran his hand through his short-cropped salt-and-pepper hair, and moved to the center of the pitch. The boys followed, all of them hopping up and down, excited about the prospects of making the team.

Ian Marshall, club Chairman and the other co-manager, walked the touchline, keeping his eye on the middle where the boys congregated. His beard was 3-days old and he wished he hadn't eaten that big lunch. He paced back and forth. He knew all too well that future stars did not grow on trees, but they did come to tryouts and new talent was the lifeblood of Ridgeway. They were a grassroots club and had a good track record over the years. It didn't hurt that David Beckham played here. It drew kids from all over London.

Harry trotted out to greet Bricknell in the circle and joined the rest of the boys. He was the smallest one.

"My name is Dave Bricknell," he announced and the boys instantly lined up in front of him. "You can call me Mr. Bricknell. Now, do you know why we're here?"

A couple hands went up and Bricknell pointed to a tall boy.

"To learn how to play," the boy said.

"Obviously," Bricknell said. "But more importantly, to learn how to play in a team and lastly, to have fun." He scanned the boys and smiled. "So you are here for some fun. I insist. Anyone disagree?"

No hands went up.

"If you are fortunate enough to make it here, your training will be run by Mr. Ian Marshall, the Chairman of the Ridgeway Rovers FC. Do you know what you will call Mr. Ian Marshall?" he called on the same tall boy, whose hand shot up.

"Mr. Marshall?"

"Exactly," Bricknell replied with a grin. "We hold tryouts here at Loughton, but we train at Peter May Sports Centre."

Harry peeked at him through two tall boys.

"Time to pick squads. We want to get a look at you in action. I always choose the keeper first. Which one of you is a keeper?" He looked around the crowd of boys. No hands shot up this time.

"Don't tell me you're all strikers!"

That is when he saw a hand go up from behind the rest of the boys. "You," he said.

The boys parted, revealing the smallest boy out there: Harry.

"I'll have a go at it," Harry said.

Bricknell stepped over to him. "Ever played in goal before?"

Harry grinned. "My big brother Charlie makes me play it all the time. I hate it. He's bigger than me. But I always get him. I stop them all. Being a goalie is not what I *want* to do. I want to *score* goals. But if you need a goalie, I'll do it."

Bricknell burst out laughing. "See?" he said, smiling at Harry. "Here's a boy who knows how to have fun!"

Harry smiled. It felt good.

"That's what I like to hear, son," Bricknell said. "There's the kit over there. Grab some gloves and let's see what you can do – what's your name?"

"Harry. Harry Kane."

"Harry Kane, like a hurricane," Bricknell said. "I like it. Take that goal," he said, pointing to the net closest to him.

"Yes, sir," Harry nodded and made his way to the goal.

That's when Bricknell saw Kim charging this way across the field. "Uh-oh, here we go," he said to Marshall. "Looks like mom isn't happy."

Kim walked right up to Bricknell. "If I could have a word," she said, dripping with politeness.

"Of course, madam," Bricknell replied. He was used to it. It happened all the time.

"My son, over there, Harry," she said, pointing. "I saw you talking to him. Harry is not a goalie. He's outfield."

Bricknell smiled back. "Of course, madam. Don't worry, he'll get a go in all positions. You should be proud. He was brave enough and kind enough to volunteer as a keeper when no one else would. We are grateful for his enthusiasm."

Kim blushed. "Well, thank you, sorry to have bothered you, you probably get that all the time. My son, well, he is a terrific player," she said.

"Yes ma'am, of course he is," Bricknell said and she smiled, then turned on her heel and trotted off the field.

Harry stood at the goal line. When his eyes met Bricknell's, he winked.

Bricknell laughed and slapped Marshall's back. "Did you see that?"

Later, Bricknell played Harry at the top, and by the end of the match, the boy had scored a hat trick, winning the match for his side.

"Did I make it, coach?" Harry asked as he left the field victoriously, surrounded by his mates.

"What do you think?"

"I hope I did," Harry said.

Bricknell grinned. "You hoped right," he said and Harry smiled broadly.

He liked the kid.

CHAPTER 4
WINTER AT RIDGEWAY

It was a freezing cold winter morning. In fact, it was so cold, Harry could see his breath. But nothing would stop him from playing soccer.

He measured out some strides down the road in front of his house then stopped.

"Right here," he said, pulling off his jacket and laying it down on one side of the line down the middle of the road. His friend, Dave, laid his jacket on the other side. That marked one set of goalposts. A bunch of boys down the road about a field's-length, did the same. Everything was ready for the pick-up game. Five-a-side. The perfect start of a day for eight-year-old Harry and his friends, George, Nick, Kevin, and Dave.

Playing here, he had to keep his shots low so even if it hit his neighbor's wall, it would miss the window. He dribbled lightning fast down the narrow street, steam billowing out with every breath, like a train, steering clear of all marauding players from the other side. He was smaller than the others, but they still struggled to keep up. Harry loved every minute of it. Didn't matter if it was at recess or lunch at school, training with Ridgeway in the afternoons, or just plain old street ball.

"Keep it low! Keep it low!" Dave shouted.

The other boys came at Harry like a line of giant killer toads and stayed tight on him.

So, Harry lobbed the ball to David, who scored before the other team knew what'd hit them.

"Cheat!" the biggest toad said.

Harry stopped playing and stomped over to him and got in his face. More or less. He was a lot shorter than the biggest toad so he had to look up. "How is that cheating?! Every time we score, you yell *cheat*!?"

The head toad stopped in his tracks and looked around. Everyone waited for his answer.

A light dusting of snow started to fall and turned everything white, including all the boys' heads.

"Well," the head toad hesitated and shrugged.

"Yes, Mr. Toad?!" Harry said, growing impatient, and the boys giggled.

"Well, that's what they do in Europe!"

No one said a word for a split-second, then Harry burst out laughing, and the rest of the boys joined in. Harry draped his arm over his friend's shoulders. "Well, this is England, mate! Where we do things right!"

George checked his watch. "We got five minutes till first bell everyone!" he shouted. They all scrambled, threw on their jackets, grabbed their bags, and charged in a herd to their school, a couple blocks away.

In the early afternoon, Harry took the bus to Peter May Sports Centre on Wadham Road in Walthamstow. As the double-decker bounced along, he quietly took his red Ridgeway home team jersey from his kit and pulled it on. His team shorts were on under his pants and by the time the bus came to a complete stop, he was ready to play. He shouldered his kit and hurriedly exited down the steel stairs, his studs clicking, and hopped onto the curb as the bus roared away behind him, splattering the back of his neck with bits of freezing cold snow.

Minutes later, Harry weaved through the cones, the ball close to his foot. He lost his rhythm and stumbled over the ball and landed face down in the cold grass. He got up, his face burning slowly to frustration. He glanced at the touchline.

The coaches were all in a line, watching his every move.

He shrugged, then trotted back to the top of the cones and started again. He was just getting to the end when he lost his rhythm a second time and once more fell on his face. It hurt. He felt the pain and the pinching cold and the frustration boiling up inside him.

But he didn't give up. He had to do it again, until he could do it right. And he knew that by the end of these boring drills, he'd get to play and just the thought of it made him happy. This was all he ever wanted to do, forever.

CHAPTER 5
ARSENAL

Out on the Ridgeway field in Chingford, Harry cut into the box as Andros sent him a cross. With a perfect touch, Harry headed it into the goal. He was the smallest on the pitch and was instantly engulfed by his teammates who surrounded him and bounced around the field in unison, tightly clinging to each other in celebration.

Pat and Kim Kane leaped to their feet in the stands along with the other parents and friends. Kim noticed a couple of men nearby, furiously scribbling notes on pads of paper. "What's that all about?" she asked.

Pat studied the men and grinned. He had seen them before over the years. "Scouts. From the Premier League," he said a little too loudly. The men looked up when they heard him. He shrugged back at them and felt himself blush. They nodded and went back to watching the game and scribbling their notes.

Down on the field, the match ended and as Harry walked off, he was joined by Ian Marshall and Dave Bricknell. Ian put his arm over Harry's shoulders. "Well done, Harry."

"Nice goal," Bricknell chimed in.

"Thank you, sir," Harry replied.

"How many is that for the season?" Bricknell asked.

"Seventeen, I believe," Harry said.

"Eighteen, actually," Ian said. "Eighteen goals in fifteen games." He beamed at the boy.

Harry flashed a grin, then got a worried look on his face. "I can do better!"

The men laughed. But Harry was serious.

"Your father here?" Ian asked.

Harry froze. "Yes, he's over there," he pointed to the stands. "A-Am I in trouble?"

Bricknell chuckled. "Not unless you think eighteen goals in fifteen games is bad," he said.

Harry blushed. "I guess not."

"Do us a favor and let your dad know we want to speak with him." Marshall said, and he and Bricknell turned and walked away.

Harry rushed off to his parents in the stands and told his father what Mr. Marshall had said. Pat got up and came down to join Harry. He started to walk across the grounds and Harry followed. Pat turned back. "Go and get changed, son," he said. "I'll deal with this."

Harry nodded and scampered off to the changing room. Pat looked across the field. Ian waved him over.

Moments later, the two men and Bricknell watched the older squads go through their paces. "I'll get straight to the point, Mr. Kane," Ian said. "The Arsenal scout was here."

Pat was surprised.

"He wants to see Harry at their next tryout."

Pat thought about it for a moment and mouthed the word, "Arsenal?" He was not enthusiastic and Ian nodded. "As you probably know," Pat went on, "we're Spurs."

"And?" Bricknell asked with a chuckle.

Pat smiled at them. "I thought it was worth mentioning. But of course, we want what's best for Harry, don't we? After all, he's only eight."

"He's one of our best," Ian replied, wondering what Harry's dad was on about. "Something bothering you?"

"Well, it's just that – it wouldn't ruin it for him here, would it? He's having so much fun."

So that was it, Ian thought. *He's worried he'll leave us and never get back.* He softened his smile. "Let him see how it goes, Mr. Kane. Our door is always open for Harry. He can come back to Ridgeway any time if it doesn't pan out."

Pat looked relieved. "But what if he *doesn't* make the grade? I don't want to get his hopes up."

Ian smiled. "I know where you're coming from. As a father. But Harry is a strong-willed kid with talent. Give him a shot. Let him go to the tryout."

Pat nodded. *Arsenal?* He thought about how he should bring up the news and knew it wouldn't be easy.

He told Harry on the way home. Harry's blue eyes grew wide.

"We hate Arsenal!" he blurted out and Pat and Kim chuckled.

"I know. But it was an Arsenal scout who spotted ya," Pat said.

"I'm not joking," Harry said.

"Hate's a strong word, Harry," Kim scolded.

"I know what you mean, son, but Arsenal is the second-best team in England right now."

Harry wasn't happy. "But you only taught me to love the Spurs!"

It was true. If it had been a team from another city it would be easier. But Arsenal were the Spurs' arch rivals.

Pat and Kim waited on tenterhooks while Harry tore open an energy snack. "We'll need an answer, love," Kim said.

Harry seemed to be ignoring them.

After a couple of bites, he looked up and grinned. "I'll do it."

Pat and Kim relaxed.

"Maybe it will help me move up to a higher level," Harry said.

The day of the Arsenal trials, Harry put on his Spurs jersey and stood defiantly in front of the full-length mirror.

Kim walked by. "Uh, no, I think not," she said and kept walking.

Harry slouched a little in the mirror.

"Don't tempt fate, Harry!" she shouted from the other room.

Harry grinned. *Why are moms always right?*

It was a half an hour drive from Chingford to London Colney in Hertfordshire, the Arsenal training ground. Harry plastered his face against the car window as they got off the M25 and approached the massive grounds. "Whoa!" Harry marveled. The buildings were modern with the red Arsenal flag flying out front. Behind the building complex were the grounds, 10 perfect-sized pitches: two to the left as they walked in and eight in front of them in two rows of four each.

Harry walked through to where the U9 tryouts were to be held. He was amazed. His eyes were wide as saucers.

"Oh, Harry, will you look at that," Pat marveled.

Once Pat found a seat in the stands, Harry trotted down to the touchline and stopped to take it all in. He stood next to another boy his own age, who smiled at him. "Nico," the boy said, "Yennaris."

"Harry Kane," Harry answered.

"Hey, that's my middle name," Nico said without taking his eyes off the pitch.

Harry looked at him. "What, Kane?"

Nico giggled. "No, Harry. Harry. Harold actually."

On the field, the youth coach, Steve Leonard, stood next to a paper sign with *U9* scrawled on it in black marker pen. A handful of boys were already lined-up.

"That's my group!" Harry said, pointing to the U9 boys. "Nice meeting you." He started to trot across the field. Nico charged after him and caught up, matching his pace.

"Mine too," Nico grinned.

The tryouts consisted of drills and more drills.

"When do we get to shoot?" Harry whispered to Nico, nervously bouncing from one foot to the other.

At that moment, as if in answer to his wishes, Steve Leonard announced the shooting portion of the tryouts. He lined the boys up by height and so Harry, being the shortest, was last.

Nico went just before him. Harry thought he showed a lot of good skill in his kick. When he was finished, it was Harry's turn.

Harry high-fived his newfound friend. "Nailed it," Nico whispered. Harry nodded then focused on the job at hand. He was already busy doing what he always did to prepare for a free kick, the kind of thing that drove all his soccer mates crazy. He studied the cut of the grass. The goalie. The grass again. The goalie again.

"Kane!" the coach shouted. "You're up." He tossed Harry a ball. "Three shots."

Harry grinned and let the ball drop. He bent it into the left corner, completely fooling the keeper. And he did it again and again. He scored three out of three.

The goalie glared at him in disbelief. The short kid was good.

Everyone cheered.

Leonard smiled as Harry rejoined the boys. "Well done!" he said. "You're in."

Harry took a deep breath and looked over at Nico, who gave him the thumbs up. He was in too.

It was the best moment in eight-year-old Harry's life. Arsenal asked him to stay for the season, and he loved every minute of it. He played well and he felt as if he was on the top of the world. He loved the training sessions. He enjoyed playing with his teammates. His future with Arsenal looked bright.

CHAPTER 6
SETBACK

Harry sat at the kitchen table with his head down on his arms, hiding his face, sobbing. The letter from Arsenal that informed him he wasn't invited to their next season was open on the table. Charlie came in and put his hand on his younger brother's shoulder to comfort him and Harry struck out, batting him away like a pesky fly. "Leave me alone," Harry said.

Charlie looked down at his brother. "Not a chance."

He grabbed Harry by the back of his shirt, pulling him to his feet. "We're going for a walk."

Harry's eyes were red and his face was streaked with tears. He slowly turned his head and looked up at his brother and decided to give up the fight. "Whatever."

The air was still cold and the streets were wet from the morning rain. Charlie held an open umbrella over his head even though it wasn't raining. They walked briskly around the neighborhood. Harry stayed on the other side of the sidewalk from Charlie and wouldn't get under the umbrella. Neither of them said a word for blocks, till Harry felt like exploding. "I was good and I scored lots of goals," he finally blurted out. "I don't want to play in clubs anymore."

Charlie looked at him, long and hard. "Mom and Dad didn't teach you to be a quitter."

"I'm not a quitter," Harry replied.

"Coulda fooled me. How about perseverance? You got that?"

Harry stared dumbly at his big brother. "I don't even know what that means," he said.

"It means, you never quit. You never give up."

Harry's eyes met his brother's and he looked away.

"I thought you wanted to be a pro. I thought you wanted to succeed."

"More than anything," Harry replied.

"Then grow up! So what if they dumped you. It's their loss."

Harry thought about it. He did feel like nobody wanted him. He was always taught to be honest, especially with himself. This was one of those times. "Well, I wasn't the best player, Charlie, but I wasn't the worst. They said I was too small."

"And chubby," Charlie added.

"I'm not!" Harry cried out. But he knew it was true.

"Look, you're going to grow. Someday, you'll be taller than me. And you'll be the player that everyone wants. As long as you don't quit. And then they'll be sorry, won't they?" Charlie said.

Harry nodded. "I suppose. Yeah. They will."

It started to rain but Harry didn't budge and let it wash over him.

Charlie moved the umbrella over toward his brother. Harry scooted under. Out of the rain, it was time to move on from the pain. He was almost nine. "Do you think the Rovers still want me?"

Charlie smiled. "Let's find out."

Pat drove the boys to the Peter May Sports Centre the same day. Ian Marshall saw Harry out of the corner of his eye the moment he stepped out on the field, and smiled to himself. Instead of walking over to greet the boy, he joined the U10 squad who were ready for their training session. He stood among the boys, not saying a word. And waited.

Harry wasn't sure what to do, so he trotted out to the group and joined them. Ian still had his back to the boys. He turned slowly around and noticed Harry. He nodded to him. "Okay," he said. "New season. New plans. I think we've got everyone we need."

Harry's heart sunk.

"All we're missing is a fox in the box. We need someone who will score goals. You boys know anybody that fits that description?"

Harry couldn't believe it. He waved his hand wildly. "Me! Yeah me! Me!"

"Who's *me*?"

"It's me, Mr. Marshall, don't you remember?! Harry Kane!"

Ian walked over to Harry and eyeballed him. "Well, I have to admit, you do look familiar," he said and craned his head around and winked to the other boys.

The boys giggled.

Harry blushed. "I can score goals, Mr. Marshall."

Ian grinned broadly. "Well, in that case, welcome home, Harry."

CHAPTER 7

CHINGFORD & BECKHAM

Harry spent the next two years going to school at Larkspur Primary in East London and playing for Ridgeway, making a name for himself. When he turned 11, he started a new school, closer to home, The Chingford Foundation. That's where he saw *her* on the first day of class; saw her as if for the first time. She had gone to Larkspur as well, but Harry hadn't really registered she was in the same year. She moved up to Chingford when he did.

There she was. He and his older brother Charlie walked through the front doors and she was standing in the main hall, staring up at the jersey hanging on the wall, signed by David Beckham. Becks had been a Chingford Foundation student as a boy and his father was one of the soccer coaches. It was Chingford's claim to fame.

Katie Goodland was with a couple of friends, talking, and Harry noticed that where she was once short and plain, she was now tall and athletic and had a friendly smile.

He stopped and stared at her because he knew it would be hard to get a good look it he was moving too fast. When she looked over, he quickly looked up at the Beckham jersey and Charlie, coming up unawares behind him, slammed into him, almost knocking him over.

"What are you doing, Harry?! Move!" Charlie said and shoved his younger brother on ahead of him.

Katie noticed him approaching and smiled. "Hi, Harry," she said.

To Harry, her voice was pure music and as they continued walking to their first day of class, Harry snuck one last look at her as they passed. She smiled back. "Go Spurs!" she said, pointing to his bag.

He blushed. The Tottenham logo was sprayed all over it.

Later that day, he felt something magical happen when she sat down next to him in class.

"I'll bet you didn't know I was a big Spurs fan," she said with a grin.

Harry froze, unable to speak for a moment. "I-I didn't," he finally got out.

"There's school team tryouts at lunch. Are you going?"

Harry nodded dumbly.

She smiled. "Best in London," she said. "Only the best for Harry Kane, eh?" she continued and scurried away.

Harry was shocked she remembered his whole name.

The cheering from the field could be heard all over the school. It looked as if most of the student body had turned out to watch the tryouts.

Harry stood on the touchline, suited up in shorts, boots, and a Chingford Foundation maroon and gold PE kit. Charlie stood next to him. "Think you can make the team?" Charlie asked.

"They'll need a goal scorer, won't they?"

"*Everyone* needs a goal scorer," Charlie replied.

Harry grinned. "There you go."

"You sound pretty sure of yourself."

"Perseverance, Charlie," Harry said. "If I never give up – I'll never fail."

Charlie laughed.

"I think it was Becks who said that, wasn't it?" Harry said.

"Very funny, it was me," Charlie replied, taking another look out on the field. "Hey, there's some good players out there, little bro."

"Best in London," Harry replied.

Mark Leadon, the Chingford coach paced up and down, directing the drills, watching the boys intently. He finally glanced down the line at Harry. "Alright then," he said, pointing to the field.

Harry started to run and Charlie dragged him back for one last piece of advice. "Mr. Leadon hates a showoff," he said.

Harry gave his brother a nod. Charlie had been here at Chingford for two years and knew the ropes. Harry bumped fists with him. "I know what to do." Then he trotted out on the field to join the boys already out there, stretching. "Good luck," he said to the tall guy next to him.

"Same to you, mate," the boy grinned. "I'm Mr. Leadon's assistant."

The boys called out on the field did some passing exercises, then Harry did some dribbling. He was not very good. "You can do this," he whispered to himself when he got another try. This time he got to the box and lobbed the ball over the goalie's head into the right-hand corner, completely fooling him.

Charlie, in the stands, stood up. "Nice," he said to himself. He looked to his left, down the row of bleachers, and saw the girl Harry was getting all crazy over earlier.

Katie was excitedly on her feet. Her girlfriend stayed in her seat and pulled Katie back down. "Know him?"

Katie blushed. "Maybe," she said. "He sits next to me in class."

Her friend smiled. "So that's why it was so important to get out here."

Katie giggled.

"He's a Spurs fan," Katie said.

The other girl smirked. "Who isn't?"

They both chuckled.

Mr. Leadon liked what he saw. "Who's that?" he asked his assistant who thumbed through some pages on his clipboard. "Harry Kane. 11. Just started here. Plays for Ridgeway. Did a season with the Gunners. Also, he wished me luck."

"Well, at least he's polite, isn't he? He's small, but I like him"

"And a good runner. He just never stops, does he?" the assistant marveled.

Leadon looked at his assistant and smiled. "He's my first pick."

Leadon got everything he wanted from Harry and much more. Harry shined that first year at Chingford and led the team to their first championship in years. When he wasn't at school playing, he was playing at Ridgeway and in his spare time he played pick-up games down the road with friends. And when he wasn't kicking a ball he was studying other players on TV. The Arsenal setback was already forgotten.

He regained his self-confidence. He knew what he wanted to do.

The following year, David Beckham returned to the Chingford Foundation School, the place he attended as a boy. He was two years into his contract playing for Real Madrid and he was on top of his game; one of the best-known athletes in the world. It was time to give back, so he created The David Beckham Academy on Greenwich Peninsula near the North Greenwich Tube Station. The Chingford squads were ecstatic when he came to visit and stood in front of them on the Chingford pitch. The kids were all suited-up and lined up. Mark Leadon stood beside him. "The field is yours, sir," he said.

Beckham laughed and slapped Leadon's back. "Thanks, Mark, I always wanted to hear you call me sir!"

"I'll bet," Leadon replied. "I called you plenty of other things."

The boys took the field and went through the usual Chingford drills while Beckham watched. He noticed one boy who stood out from the rest and pointed him out. Leadon nodded and let Beckham see the notes he had on the boy.

After drills, Beckham addressed the team for a ten-minute pep-talk. He concluded with: "My father was a coach here and that's why I am here today," he said. "Now come on up, I want to meet you. All of you," he said.

All the kids formed a single-file line and one-by-one shook his hand and got to have a short conversation with him. Harry and Katie stood in line together with the rest of the team, waiting to meet the great Becks and shake his hand. "What are you going to say?" Katie asked.

Harry's eyes grew wide. "S-s-say?" he whispered back.

Katie giggled. Harry got behind her. She made a fake move toward Beckham, then quickly whipped behind Harry and suddenly Harry was staring into the smiling face of David Beckham. He stuck out his hand.

"David," he said and Harry shook his hand.

Harry forgot to let go of Beckham's hand. "H-Harry Kane, sir," Harry said.

"I hear you play for the Ridgeway Rovers?"

"Yes, sir!" *How come the great Beckham knew?!*

"They're a great club," Beckham said. "I have a question for you, Harry. What do you want more than anything?"

Harry flashed a smile. "To play at Wembley! For England! And one day at the World Cup, sir."

Beckham put his hand on Harry's shoulder. "I saw you out there today."

Harry thought he was going to faint. He just stared at the grass sheepishly.

"You know you can do it. You can get there. You know how?"

"Yes, sir," Harry said. "By never giving up."

Beckham laughed and patted him on the back. "Exactly right, Harry! And you know what? I'm looking forward to seeing you there!"

CHAPTER 8

THE SHOWDOWN

Harry saw the Range Rover first. It stood out like a glittering golden coach, never seen in these parts. He and his mates were in the middle of a pick-up game in the street and Harry's side was destroying the other. They kept playing even though the fancy car was heading up the street, aiming straight for them.

Instead of driving by, the car stopped. Harry and his mates froze and watched as two men got out, one on either side. Harry recognized one of the men immediately. It was one of his heroes: Jermain Defoe, striker for the Spurs. Harry blinked. He thought he was seeing things. Sometimes, if he and his mates snuck over to the M25, they could catch a glimpse of a Spurs team bus or a Spurs player heading to work in his fancy car, but Jermain Defoe stopping on his street and getting out and walking their way? Impossible! Yet, the man was the right height. He wasn't a tall man; he was just – great.

Jermain grinned when he and his driver stopped in front of the boys. "Who wants a game?" he asked.

The boys looked at each other but no one could say a thing. They all knew who he was.

And they didn't believe he was addressing them. It was as if seeing the man struck them mute.

Harry finally spoke up. "Uh, the Lane is another 5 miles down the road, mate."

The boys chuckled uncomfortably, but Jermain laughed out loud.

"So you're saying you're out then, *mate*?" Jermain quipped with a grin.

Harry's eyes widened and betrayed his tell-tale look. "No!" he shouted, shaking his head. Then he rushed to Jermain's side. "We're ready, Mr. Defoe! You and me against everyone else!"

The rest of the boys groaned like a ghostly choir. "Not fair!" one of the boys shouted.

Harry thought about it and winked at Jermain. "They're right. Okay, I'll take one side, you take the other."

"I take it you're the leader then," Jermain said. "What's your name?"

"Harry, sir. Harry Kane."

Jermain returned his attention to the boys as they surrounded him in a semi-circle. "Okay, guys. Harry takes one side; I'll take the other." He winked at Harry. "Five-a-side, mate. Let's see what you can do."

Harry locked eyes with Jermain, dropped the ball, and took off, followed closely by his four mates, all before Jermain could react.

"I guess I showed him," Jermain kidded with the boys on his side.

"Let's get 'em!" one of his mates said.

"You're right," Jermain said. "Let's go!" He charged after Harry and the boys. Jermain got the ball away from him in a heartbeat and scored from what seemed like a block away. As Jermain and Harry passed each other on the sidewalk, Jermain tossed the ball to Harry. "Your turn."

Harry looked at the ball. He wanted what Jermain Defoe had. He wanted what Becks had. He wanted what Teddy Sheringham had.

Before he could form another thought, Harry heard the ball whizz past his ear as it rocketed in.

Bam! Jermain had shot another goal. He turned and grinned and gave Harry a thumb's up. "You lost focus, Harry! Thanks for the goal!" All the boys on his five-man squad chuckled.

Harry scowled.

When play resumed, Harry, one-on-one with Jermain, stole the ball away from him. He dribbled down the street, carefully missing the parked cars, and slammed it into the stone-marked goal. There was no resistance from the other side. He turned as Jermain trotted up to him and high-fived him.

"Nice one," Jermain said. "You listened."

"Yes, sir," Harry said, breathless.

"Jermain," Jermain said.

"Yes, sir, Jermain," Harry said and Jermain laughed.

They played for 30 minutes, then Jermain grabbed the ball and stopped the match. "Sorry, guys, I have to go now." He tossed the ball to Harry. "You're good, Harry!" he said and trotted back to his Range Rover.

"See you at the Lane!" Harry shouted after him.

Jermain waved without looking back.

"I'll be there playing some day," Harry whispered, just loud enough that only he could hear. The rest of his friends surrounded him.

"Can you believe it?!"

"Jermain Defoe!"

"And you got one over on him, Harry!"

"Yeah, he probably let me," Harry said.

"No, he wasn't ready. I saw his face! Your goal was the real deal!"

"You think so?"

"Yes!" they all shouted. Someone grabbed the ball and stole it and headed for the goal at the far end of the street, and the game was on again.

Later that afternoon, Harry took the bus to Ridgeway. When he got to the field, he never noticed anything different about the man who had been sitting in the stands regularly for almost a year. Harry thought he was one of the owners. His name was Mark O'Toole, a youth scout for Tottenham.

Ian Marshall knew him, but rarely acknowledged him. He knew what would be coming, he had been watching for a year, off and on. He knew who he was after and he wondered what was taking him so long.

The Ridgeway Rovers were always there for Harry. Whenever he wanted to go back after a spell with another team, all he had to do was ask. It kept him humble and it was that humility that ultimately helped make him a star. He played for the school teams at the Chingford Foundation School during the day, and afternoons, his club was the Rovers. His spell with Arsenal made a name for him and that occasionally brought out the scouts. London and environs was a hot spot for superstars, present and future.

Harry was out in the street when Kim Kane came out of their house. "HAAARRRYYYY!" she shouted up the block, waving him over.

Harry watched her for a moment, wondering what she wanted.

"You better go, H," one of his friends said.

Harry nodded.

"The Golden Boys want to see you," Kim Kane said.

"*Watford* wants me?" he asked.

"They want to *see* you," she replied, ever the realist. "They're offering you a tryout."

"The Hornets are pros," she said as they walked. "Elton John is one of the owners."

"Elton who?" Harry asked with a wink.

Kim smirked. "Very funny."

"You know what I don't get, Mom," Harry said. "Their colors are yellow and black, same as hornets. But their emblem is a moose."

Kim laughed. "That's not a moose, it's a red hart. Originally, way before you were born, their emblem was a hornet. *Harry the Hornet*, actually. They changed it to a red hart because Watford is in the county of Hertfordshire. If it had been a white hart, I might have thought it was an omen instead of a tryout."

Harry grinned. "Harry the Hornet. I like that."

Three days later, Harry took the field in Hertfordshire and strutted his stuff.

An hour later, he made the team.

And became *Harry the Hornet*. The trial period would last four to six weeks, but after the first session, the Golden Boys gave him a jersey.

Back at Ridgeway, Ian Marshall and Dave Bricknell were philosophical about it when they learned from Harry that he was with Watford. The next time Mark O'Toole was there and he saw everyone but Harry, he got nervous. Instead of everyone at Ridgeway avoiding him, he went down to the first row in the stands and shouted: "Ian!"

When Ian looked up, he saw O'Toole waving him over, and took his time walking over. He knew why he was calling him. It was because Harry wasn't there. He leaned on the fence. "Mark, so nice to see you. What can I do for you?"

O'Toole smiled. "Oh, nothing much. Where's Harry Kane?" he asked.

"Kane?" Ian asked. "Which one is he?"

O'Toole raised an eyebrow, sure his old friend was having him on. "You know the one. Always keeps the first yard in his head. Knows how the game is going and always knows where to go. Scores like a maniac."

"Sorry, we don't have Teddy Sheringham playing for us, you do."

O'Toole burst out laughing.

"Maybe you're thinking of our Harry," Ian said, amused.

"Just tell me where he is, Ian," O'Toole said. "I've been watching him for almost a year."

"Yeah, Dave and I noticed. But I'm afraid you're too late," Ian said. "He's on a 30-day with Watford." There was some noise out on the field and he turned to watch the action.

O'Toole looked like he had just lost his best friend. "W-Why didn't I hear about this?"

"You think Watford is going to consult Tottenham before they make a move? Maybe you were too busy watching, when you should have been deciding," Ian said, looking around.

Mark nodded. He didn't like it one bit.

Ian smiled. "Good luck," he muttered.

Harry was the best player on his Watford youth squad the moment he made their sheet and he felt weird when, one day, he played against the Spurs. Mark O'Toole watched the match and knew what he had to do. He went to the youth coach's room for a chat.

"You know me, I like a sure thing," Mark said to the men sitting around the table in the back room.

"He's too small," one of the coaches said.

"You saw him out there," Mark replied. "He's a natural number nine."

"So we keep our eyes on him, let him grow," another coach said.

"Come on, mates, he killed us out there today," Mark said. "Harry's a dead cert. I say we bring him in for a tryout before he falls in love with Watford and they get too attached to him."

The room grew silent for a full minute. Then it was unanimous.

And that's how Harry Kane first came to the Spurs.

But at the close of his first season, he was sent that letter of release that tore his heart out. First Arsenal. Now the Spurs. This one hurt a thousand times worse. He didn't get it. He thought he'd had a great season.

Now he would have to start all over again.

CHAPTER 9

FROM BUNGLE TO BOOM

Harry crumpled the release letter from Tottenham in his fist and wadded it up into a ball, all the while watching the boys in the park play their match a short distance away. He wanted to burn it. He felt as if he had wasted his time with soccer, and Arsenal, and now the Spurs proved it. He felt cursed. What was the point in playing? He shoved the letter ball into his jacket pocket. He'd chuck it in the trash when he got home.

He had seen enough of the match in the park. He spun on his heel and reversed course on the path. When he got to the fence, he saw his father waving from the other side of the street. He couldn't tell what he was saying, he was too far away. It must be important. He was waving his arms like a madman. He always did that when it was important.

Harry trotted to him. "You want me, Dad?"

"Telephone," Pat Kane said, breathless. "For you." He was clearly excited.

Harry stared at his father, his face still streaked with tears. "Who is it?"

Pat gulped another breath. "The Spurs, son," he said. "They're saying they made a mess of the letter."

Harry didn't bother replying. He was already sprinting to the house.

Minutes later, in the warm confines of his Chingford home, Harry held the telephone receiver to his ear and listened intently while Alex Inglethorpe, the U14 coach said, "We sent you the wrong letter, Harry! I'm so sorry! I hope it's not too late!"

The wrong letter? He wasn't dropped? Harry felt like flying right then and there. He felt like squatting down and pushing off and flying up past the treetops, just like in his dreams.

Harry finally found a smile. "You mean I'm coming back?!"

Inglethorpe laughed nervously. "You never left," he said.

When they finished their conversation, Harry politely said goodbye and promised to see Mr. Inglethorpe at the academy the following day. He put the receiver back and turned to his mom and dad with the biggest smile either of them had ever seen.

"All right, what did he say?" Kim asked. "I'm dying to know!"

"*They never wanted me to leave,*" Harry replied. "I'm in."

Kim wrapped her arm over her son's shoulders. "I reckon we forgive them for their faulty paperwork." She hugged him tight. Pat just smiled broadly.

"How about you, Harry?" Pat asked his son.

"There was something else Mr. Inglethorpe said on the phone."

"Oh?" Kim said. "What's that?"

"He wants me to grow. I have to – if I want to move up to next year."

"You will," Kim said. She hoped she was right.

A week later, Harry stepped out on the Spurs youth field and joined the U14 squad as its newest member and stood between his friends Ryan Mason and Andros Townsend. Last season, together, they were a formidable scoring trio.

Alex Inglethorpe walked down the line of boys as he spoke. "My main mission here at Tottenham is to develop the U18 team, so you're probably wondering why I'm coaching the U14 squad once a week," he said. He was firm and direct. "Are you?"

No one said a word. Harry raised his hand. "Because you're looking for players who're good enough for your team?"

Inglethorpe pointed at him. "Exactly, Harry!" He stopped pacing and stood in front of them with his hands on his hips. "I'm looking for boys for my squad. And to get to *my* squad, you have to move up to U16. And to get to U16." He stopped talking and looked around the group. "To get to U16...well, you have to earn it. Who's with me?"

Everyone raised their hands.

"Good," Inglethorpe said. "Let's get to work."

Harry was an amazing student. He had a great attitude. Inglethorpe didn't think he stood out, but he knew his limits and always worked on his weaknesses. Most importantly, he did not panic.

"Although you may not get it other days with the rest of the coaches here, with me, I will always stay for extra practice," Inglethorpe said. "Anybody else?"

Harry raised his hand. In fact, he always raised his hand.

"Good. Are you going to let Harry train alone?"

A few more hands went up. Inglethorpe told the boys that hard work is more important than talent. He saw many kids with talent who were lazy and that didn't get them anywhere. He wasn't sure how talented Harry was but he knew the boy was willing to put in the hours. He was eager to learn.

Harry played well that season, but something about him bothered Inglethorpe and a few months into the season, he jogged over to the stands for a chat with Pat.

"Can we talk? About Harry?"

Pat smiled. "How can I say no to that?"

Inglethorpe smiled. "Harry has a great attitude, he's not distinctive. Yet. He seems to know his weaknesses and works on them constantly. He's my best student. He always stays late. Honestly, I can't imagine not having him here."

Pat looked at the coach. "Sounds perfect."

"Look, Mr. Kane," Inglethorpe said. "Every age group is a new challenge, you know that."

"But?" Pat interjected.

"But unless we see some real improvement, we don't think Harry will make it in the U16s."

Pat studied the coach and thought about it. "You know that already?"

Inglethorpe nodded. "He's not growing fast enough. He needs to grow so he can increase his speed."

"Well, he's going to grow," Pat said, standing up. "Guaranteed. Look at me. He's going to beat me in height eventually, that's what the doctor says."

Inglethorpe stood up. "I believe you," he said. "I just hope it's sooner rather than later."

CHAPTER 10
PERSEVERANCE

Pat Kane hired a private trainer for Harry on the recommendation of Inglethorpe. And as if the universe listened and increased the challenge, it rained almost every day while Harry trained with him.

Harry ran with all his might from the middle of the park, down the muddy path toward the other end. Rain beat against his face, but he could not slow down to wipe it away so he had to shake his head like a horse as he galloped toward his trainer at the other end of the park. He stood, well-protected from the rain, in front of a makeshift goal, holding a stopwatch.

The trainer never took his eyes off the stopwatch as the numbers flicked by.

He clicked when Harry whizzed past.

"Two seconds! You shaved another two seconds off your time!"

Harry trotted back, breathless, soaking wet. "That's fantastic! So we can take a break?"

"Harry, it was perfect," he said with a smile. "So, let's do it again."

Harry frowned and didn't move.

"Come on, Hurricane," the trainer said. "Your dad is paying big money to get you in shape. And let's face it. You're no track star."

"But you said it was perfect."

"Perfect for then. But now we've set the bar higher. Oh, and for talking back, drop and give me ten."

Harry groaned.

"Do it."

Harry dropped to the wet grass in push-up position and knocked off ten quick push-ups. When he was done, he jumped to his feet and brushed the mud off his hands. "You know at Tottenham they compare me to Jermain Defoe. I even played with him once when I was a kid."

"You're *still* a kid."

"Yeah okay, but answer me this: what is Defoe known for? Racing?"

"No," the trainer said. "Short bursts of speed."

"Right. So what am I doing with all this long distance stuff? I need to learn how to do short bursts of speed, so I can take the shot."

The trainer crossed his arms and smiled. "Can't argue with that logic! But you've got to *be* there when the ball hits the box."

"You mean, be there *first*," Harry said.

The trainer laughed. "Exactly. That's what separates the slackers from the stars, Harry. And what if the goalie beats you?"

"Then I get the rebound!"

The coach put his hands on his hips. The rain stopped. "Well, then you have a choice to make. Do we do the easy thing and get out of the rain? Or do you try to get the rebound?"

Harry grinned. "What do you mean, *try*?"

Moments later, the trainer crouched in front of the net. When Harry kicked, he stopped the ball. Harry was there in a heartbeat to snatch the rebound and chip it over his trainer's head into the goal.

"Outstanding!" the trainer shouted.

The sky exploded in a volley of thunder.

"A few more months of this and you'll be shining!"

Harry leaned against a tree and groaned, shaking the leaves above him, showering him in cold rain water. He sighed and hoped all this extra work was worth it.

It didn't take long. Less than a season and the coaching staff noticed the difference.

The weather was perfect for the practice match at Tottenham. Harry spun away from the two defenders covering him, the ball tight to his foot and as he charged down field, dribbled the ball from one foot to the other, picking his spot in the box. The opposing players were all over him, but it was like they were invisible. They couldn't catch up and by the time they caught him, he'd already shot the ball into the lower right corner of the net.

Tim Sherwood was on the sideline with Alex Inglethorpe. "Who's that?" Sherwood asked.

"Kane. My secret weapon," Inglethorpe said with a wry smile.

"You've been hiding him from me, Al," Tim scolded.

Inglethorpe smiled.

"Well, I'm going to keep my eye on him," Tim said.

"Is that a threat? Or a promise?"

Pat Kane watched the men from his usual seat in the stands and when his son started trotting off the field, he came down to meet him on the touchline. Harry hugged him and Pat looked at him. "Well, I'll be, look at that. You're taller than me! How's my boy doing?" he asked Alex, fishing for a compliment.

Inglethorpe smiled. "Well, whatever happened with that private trainer, it worked. You made it, Harry. You're moving up to U16."

Then he leaned in closer and whispered in Harry's ear. "Congratulations. You proved them all wrong."

"Thank you," Harry whispered back.

A week later, Alex Inglethorpe started Harry on the bench. Jonathan Obika was the U16's center forward.

"The bench, Mr. Inglethorpe?" Harry was devastated.

"You have to earn your place," his coach said. Harry who was used to being automatically in the starting line-up, had to learn to adjust, and his coach knew he would. He wasn't surprised to see the disappointment in his player's eyes.

Growing pains, he thought.

"Earn my place? How am I going to do that sitting on the bench?"

Inglethorpe grinned. "Up to you," he said with a wink. "Oh, I almost forgot – welcome to the team."

CHAPTER 11

NO MATTER WHERE YOU GO, THERE YOU ARE

The 2008–09 season was all about travel for the Spurs' U18 squad. They were going to Mexico and Switzerland. The Copa Chivas in Guadalajara Mexico came first and they got an additional player just in case from the U16 team.

Harry Kane.

The night before he left for Mexico, Harry couldn't sleep. Chingford was freezing cold and he was jangly with nervous energy.

He stared at the ceiling, his mind racing about what was ahead of him this coming week all the way on the other side of the world. As a boy, he had barely seen the sun stay up past ten in the Lake District up north, let alone go anywhere foreign, and now he was flying over to Mexico.

The bedroom door creaked open and yellow chevrons of light streamed in from the hallway. Before he could react, he bounced into the air as his older brother Charlie dove onto the bed, sending him flying. Harry caught the covers to keep from tumbling to the floor and started to scream in surprise when Charlie slapped his hand over his mouth.

"Shhhh, it's me," Charlie said.

"What do you want, I'm trying to sleep!"

"No, you're not," Charlie replied. "You're wide awake. You're too excited."

Harry grinned. His brother was right. "Whatever, what do you want?"

"I have some advice before you get on that plane," Charlie whispered.

"Okay," Harry said. "What is it?"

"Don't be selfish. Help out your teammates. The game's more than just scoring. You gotta be humble."

"Come on, Charlie. You know how hard it is being humble when you're such a great guy!"

Harry kept a straight face and it took Charlie a moment to get his brother's joke. Then he burst out laughing and grabbed a pillow and threw it at him, knocking him off the bed. Harry landed on the floor with a thud that shook throughout the house.

"Are we good?" Charlie asked, helping his brother to his feet. "Don't be a ball hog. And no matter what, *don't make things worse*!"

Harry hugged him. "I won't. Love you, bro."

The next day, Harry had an aisle seat in the middle of the plane as it took off from Heathrow and turned its nose westward. He was terrified and nervously gripped the armrests. A flight attendant checked on him. "Enjoying your flight, sir?" she asked.

It was the first time anyone had addressed him as sir. "Sort of," he forced out, also forcing a follow-up smile. He wished his dad was with him. He was on his own for the first time in his life.

It was a long 15-hour flight to Guadalajara with one stop in Houston, Texas, and Harry decided to read up on where he was going before he fell asleep.

Fausto Prieto was one of Mexico's greatest goalkeepers. He was born in 1908 and played for Club Deportivo Guadalajara and the Jalisco National Team. In his honor, the Guadalajara Sports Club named a field after him at the club's facilities in Verde Valle.

The blast of Mexican desert air enveloped Harry as he disembarked. Once too short to do any good, he was now one of the tallest on his side. He boarded the maroon and white private bus that would take the squad to their quarters. The dry heat would take some getting used to. His mind raced. All he could think of were the upcoming matches, and how to get into the last eight.

The Spurs' U18 side included Steven Caulker at the back, Ryan Mason in midfield, and Andros

Townsend on the wing. Harry was one of the center forwards. They added him to the U18 squad because of a scoring tally of 22-goals in the season. Ryan Mason was top scorer and he had been challenging Harry all season. Mexico was no exception.

The Jalisco Stadium in Guadalajara was the third largest Mexican soccer stadium behind Estadio Azteca and Estadio Olimpico Universitario. It held just a little over 55,000 spectators and in Tottenham's opening salvo in the Chivas Cup facing Guadalajara in a late afternoon match, the place was overflowing.

In all, there were twenty-four sides of the best youth teams from all around the world, competing in the best tournament in the Americas. Tottenham Hotspur was there for the first time. There was Monterey, Guadalajara, Morelia, and Cruz Azul from Mexico, Saprisa from Costa Rica, Curitiba from Brazil, Club Nacional from Paraguay, Caracas FC from Venezuela, and Real Madrid from Spain.

All the sides marched in like it was the Olympics and Harry proudly matched step with his squad of older boys for the entire stadium to see. His hands were wet with sweat from the humidity and he felt it run down his back. He was definitely not in the UK anymore.

Tottenham won their first three matches and made it into third place. Harry scored 3 in the final 8 matches.

Ryan Mason who scored four goals sat next to Harry on the ride back home. He flashed four fingers. "Beat that, beanpole," he joked.

Harry narrowed his eyes. "It's not over, Mr. Mason," he said.

Ryan smiled and closed his eyes. "Wake me up when you see Big Ben."

When the team got off the plane, Kim and Pat and Charlie were waiting for him. "What's that on your skin?" Charlie asked touching Harry's reddened cheek.

"It's called a sunburn," Harry replied. "You see, in Mexico, the sky is blue and the sun burns your skin if you stay out too long in it. For instance, playing soccer all day, every day."

Pat raised an eyebrow. "Blue, you say? I've seen that once or twice in my life. I believe it was in the late 90s." They all laughed and got on the escalator down to the parking garage. Harry breathed in deep. The air smelled like fried cod and gasoline. It was perfect. He was home.

A few months later, Harry was on a plane to Switzerland. The Tottenham U18 squad competed in the *Torneo Internazionale in Bellinzona*, an

Easter tournament that had run every year since 1941 from the end of March to the beginning of April.

The first Thursday, Harry sat on the bench and watched his squad beat the pants off Club Guarani. They were up 2-0 with not much time left.

"I'm feeling strong, Mr. Inglethorpe," Harry said to his coach as he paced by, his eyes glued to the field where his team was winning.

"Not this time, H," Alex said.

That night, Harry slept in the fanciest hotel room he had ever seen. Everything was gold. Even the faucets were gold. He barely slept and woke up with a start before dawn, out of breath. At the pitch, this time against Team Ticino, he sat on the bench again.

Inglethorpe was pacing and noticed Harry's eyes drilling a hole in his back.

"Not yet, H," he said before Harry could say a word. Harry closed his eyes in frustration.

The Spurs won, 2-1.

Then, on Saturday, after winning two, it all fell apart when they faced Dinamo Bucharest.

Harry sat yet again on the bench as the squad shuffled off the field after their 1-0 loss, slapping their hands as they brushed past him. Harry followed last. "We're not out," he muttered to goalie Mirko Ranieri as they plodded into the changing room. "Thanks to you. Great saves."

"Thanks," Mirko replied.

Coach Alex went to the front of the changing room to talk to the team. "It was a scrappy game and scrappy performance, boys, so don't feel bad. We didn't create much. We huffed and puffed but there just weren't a lot of chances today. We qualified with two, but we wanted to win all three, didn't we?"

The team nodded and mumbled in agreement. They were down. He needed to bring them up.

"Conditions weren't great, Mr. Inglethorpe," Jake Nicholson, the center-back said.

"No, but we could have adapted better, right?"

"Right," some of the players said.

"I'll tell you what today's match is. It's a wake-up call. But it wasn't all bad.

Silence for a moment.

What was good about it?" Alex asked, looking from face to face.

"Mirko," Harry shouted.

Alex pointed at him. "Right!"

Everyone agreed.

"Tremendous saves!" Alex said, looking directly at the goalkeeper.

The team broke out in a loud cheer.

Then Alex paused for a moment and wiped the back of his glistening neck. "We also face the group two winner." He chuckled to himself and a wall of boys' voices filled the room. "Frankly, we've always somehow managed to miss playing each other. But not this time. It will be a great test for us. We're going up against one of the best. Barça!"

All the boys cheered, totally pumped up, their loss a distant memory.

Alex grinned and in all the excitement, Harry caught his eye and nodded with a grin.

Alex nodded back.

The next day, he put Harry in. In the 31st minute along with Oyenuga and Yaser Kasim at the front.

Harry thought his chest was going to burst when the ball was flicked to him. He instantly saw space all the way to the box and kept it close to his foot as he zig-zagged through the Barcelona players. He knew he could finish it up. Then he saw Kudus Oyenuga in perfect position. He had to give it up. It was too perfect. Without hesitation, he set it up for his teammate, who drove the ball to the back of the net and the Spurs were up 1-0.

That was the final score and when the whistle blew, Harry was instantly surrounded by his teammates, congratulating him, for his perfect pass and for being a team player.

Harry applauded the fans in the stands as he headed for the tunnel with the rest of the squad and remembered what Charlie had told him just before he left for Mexico. He chuckled to himself. "Okay, Charlie," he said to himself. "You got to me."

Then he disappeared in the tunnel, surrounded by his happy teammates.

Happy, because they were going to the final against Sporting Lisbon where Harry set up both goals and they won 2-1 and brought the trophy home.

When it was all said and done and they were on the plane back to England, Harry could have sworn he felt humble. Just like Charlie said he should.

A few weeks later, on the Spurs training field, John McDermott, the head of the Academy, watched Harry warm down. When the boys were finished, they walked off the field.

"Harry!" McDermott shouted to him as he ran by.

Harry stopped and turned to see McDermott trotting over to him. "Yes, sir?"

"We need to talk."

Harry looked at him. He hoped it was good news.

McDermott smiled at him. "I just wanted to know what you were doing next Tuesday."

Harry thought about it, then said: "It's my birthday. I'll be 16."

McDermott grinned. "I know. We were wondering, since it *is* your birthday, whether you'd have a few minutes to sign your scholarship contract."

Harry looked at him with wide eyes. He couldn't breathe for a moment.

"Yes, sir. Of course I c-can," he said trying to hold back his feelings.

"It's the club's birthday gift to you," McDermott said. "You deserve it. Happy Birthday, Harry."

CHAPTER 12

THE NEW SEASON

Alex Inglethorpe checked his watch. The rest of the U18 side were already lined-up on the grass at midfield for their season picture.

Harry ran through the clubhouse faster than anyone had seen him run before.

"Where's the fire, Harry?" one of the players asked.

"I'm late," he said. Tall and skinny, he charged out of the door, onto the pitch, and sprinted for midfield. Breathless, he saw Inglethorpe waving him over. He skidded to a stop and tried to take his place with the guys in the front row. Inglethorpe snapped his fingers and pointed to the back row. "No, Harry, not yet. But you're finally tall enough for the back row."

The squad laughed. Harry too, but he was uncomfortable and embarrassed. He forced a smile and got over the sting and Inglethorpe noticed. "Why the happy face?"

Harry sucked in a deep breath and took his place in the back row, then tongue in cheek grinned at his coach. "Because, Mr. Inglethorpe, no matter where I stand, I'm still playing for my favorite club!"

What he wanted to say was: I miss my friends. Ryan, Andros, and Steven.

They were all on loan.

Alex studied the boy. He had come a long way. He was getting better as a player and always kept his sense of humor. And even more importantly, his modesty.

He knew exactly what was bothering him.

"We count on you, Harry," the coach said.

Harry just stood there looking at him. This was serious. He felt the gravity of the situation. Deep down inside, he knew he could deliver. Still, the responsibility was huge. He had to work harder.

A month later, Harry stomped off the field with teammate Kudus, head down in shame. "Four matches and no score," Harry muttered. He was devastated. "Four in a row and nilled every time. Maybe I lost it."

Kudus punched his shoulder. "Get over it, you can't force these things."

Tom Carroll trotted up, having heard it all. "Stop trying so hard, H," he said. "Lighten up. The goals will come."

Harry draped his arm over Tom's shoulders. "Thanks, mate," he said. "You sound like my brother."

"Everyone has a dry spell," Tom assured him and Harry knew he was right.

The bad mood was over and, as it happens, Harry scored two days later, against Fulham.

Then in the next match, two more against Watford from set pieces goals.

In the changing room, Harry pulled on his street clothes.

"Great match, Harry," someone said as he was about to leave the locker room.

"Thanks," Harry said and bent over to tie his shoes.

He felt a shadow engulf him and looked up and his eyes widened. "Mr. Redknapp!"

Harry Redknapp, the first team manager, sat down opposite him. "We need to talk," he said.

Harry hated it when someone said *we need to talk*. It usually ended badly. It was just something he always expected, because of Arsenal and Tottenham. His father said he was *gun-shy*. But he also knew he had to get over it, so instead of expecting the worst, he took a deep breath and tried to think good thoughts.

"You were good out there," Redknapp said and let his every word hang in the air. He was about to change Harry's life forever. "That's what I want to talk to you about. I want you as a sub for our League Cup against Everton."

Harry could hear his heartbeat. He took a while to find the words. "You want me on the first team?"

"You've earned it, Harry," Redknapp said.

The manager left and Harry started to breathe again. His dream of playing with the Spurs was about to come true. He knew he would start on the bench and he wouldn't mind it. He called his parents and then Charlie, and broke the news. They were ecstatic.

Two weeks later, Harry sat on the bench, trying to hide the permanent scowl on his face. He wanted to be out there. He was wrong about the bench. He didn't want to sit on the bench. He wanted to be out there on the pitch. He wanted to scream it to Mr. Redknapp.

Jermaine Jenas sat at the other end of the bench. "Looks like it's just not your day," he said, looking up at the clock.

"I don't care," Harry said.

"Really?" Jenas said. "Tell that to your face."

Harry laughed. "Well, I guess it's better than it was. I mean, tell me, how was I in training?"

Jenas grinned. "I would've put you in."

"There you go," Harry stated. "I just trained with Jermaine Jenas and he said I was good enough to play!"

Jenas laughed and shoved Harry off the bench.

Christmas 2009 was the first white Christmas in England in five years. It was also a time of celebration for Harry Kane. He was doing what he loved: playing for the Spurs. When Harry came home, Kim waved an envelope in his face.

"For you," Kim said, grinning.

"Who's this from?"

She handed it to him. "Katie." She turned and walked away into the kitchen.

Harry held the envelope with both hands and stared at it, dumbfounded.

"What's she say?" Kim shouted from the kitchen.

Harry spun and charged off for his bedroom without another word.

"Harry?" Kim shouted again and looked up. Harry was gone.

Once in his room, he tore the envelope open. It was a Christmas card and a short letter from Katie Goodland. He hadn't seen her or spoken with her since she went away to college. The letter said she reads all the newspapers looking for stuff on him. *London is such a footie-mad place!* She mentioned she'd been saving all his clippings. There weren't that many yet, but she knew in her heart there would be tons soon. She signed-off the letter in the usual way: "Go Spurs!"

He folded the letter and stuffed it back in the envelope. That's when he saw the small color photo he hadn't noticed before. He snatched it up. It was a recent snapshot of her. She didn't look like a young girl anymore. She almost looked grown up. She always made him laugh and he chuckled to himself. He looked around the room figuring out what to do with the snap. Then, he opened his Tottenham kit bag and put the photo in one of the small inside pockets where he could always find it.

Summers usually went by fast and winters dragged on. This time, January 2010 came quickly. First, the Spurs lost at home to Portsmouth in the FA Youth Cup and Harry stood in the middle of the half-frozen field and held back the tears. Then, the following week, they were nilled by the MK Dons.

Harry took the lead in the locker room where the mood was grim.

"It's Coventry City next for the Premier Academy League," he announced to his teammates as they changed.

"Yeah? So?" Ku1dus Oyenuga shouted from where he was dressing.

"I just wanted to let you know that that will be the official end of our losing streak."

The boys all chuckled. "Harry's a psychic, didn't you know?" Dean Parrett said.

Harry blazed into the match and scored two in the beginning of the first half.

Kudus Oyenuga scored, Mpoku scored, and Jake Nicholson scored the fifth after 32 minutes. Finally, just before the half, Dean Parrett got a single on the board and at half-time, the Spurs were up 6-0.

Harry sat on the bench in the locker room at half time with a towel over his head, thinking about the lead, trying to keep from getting too cocky. When he looked up, the rest of the squad were lined-up in front of him. In unison, they dropped to one knee and bowed their heads.

"What's all this then?" Harry chuckled.

"We will never doubt you again, oh great sage!" Jamie Butler said.

For the second half of the match, they slowed down, but that didn't mean it was boring. Mpoku shot a low cross from the left that Harry lobbed into the net after just three minutes, earning himself a hat-trick.

Then Coventry dug in and Cyrus Christie drilled one and put the team on the scoreboard. But the Spurs went on to score an eighth goal and the U18 losing streak was officially over.

Harry went on to score another 5 goals before February rolled around.

John McDermott handed Harry the U18 captain's armband. "Put it on," he said.

Harry quickly slipped the armband over his jersey.

"Nine goals, Harry," McDermott said. "Top U18 scorer. Congratulations, Captain."

The team cheered wildly.

"Thank you, Mr. McDermott," Harry said.

"Alex always had a good feeling about you. He knew what none of the rest of us knew. And he was right," McDermott said. "Oh! I almost forgot!" He fished around in his coat and pulled out a letter. "This came for you." He handed the letter to Harry.

Harry's eyes widened. He looked from McDermott to his squad, stopping on Vedran.

"Open it," Vedran said.

Harry nodded and tore open the envelope and read the letter, then looked up in disbelief.

"Who's it from, Harry?" Vedran Corluka asked.

"J-John Peacock," Harry replied. "England U17. They're calling me up." He could barely breathe. "To Portugal. For the Algarve Tournament."

"Well deserved, Harry. Welcome to the Three Lions," McDermott said with a wide smile.

CHAPTER 13

THREE LIONS & THE LOAN RANGER

Harry was sick as a dog with the flu. He was so weak he could barely push the button on the television remote to turn up the volume, watching the U17 European Championships in Liechtenstein. It made him sicker knowing that he wasn't there with his England U17 teammates since he had worked so hard to help them qualify for the finals.

Charlie kept his distance from his younger brother. "Don't breathe on me," he said.

Harry's head throbbed. He took a sip of water. "I can't believe I'm not there. I should be there."

They continued to watch together as Harry's squad beat the pants off Spain. It was wonderful to watch, yet hard to take because Harry wanted to be there so bad. He was beyond disappointed.

The last few months had been a whirlwind of playing and achieving his goals. He was proud to join the England U17 squad for the prestigious Algarve Tournament in Portugal. All the other players had been together for more than a year. Peacock's plan was to play him behind the striker.

The Three Lions opened the tournament playing against France at Estadio Municipal Bela Vista in Portugal. Going out of the tunnel, Harry stared down at the logo on his jersey. There were three blue lions, roaring, stacked atop each other, corralled in blue on a white shield, surrounded by ten roses.

He marveled that he was really here. He was wearing the England national soccer team shirt for the first time and it felt great. He was happy to take the field for the first time against France along with Benik Afobe from Arsenal, Ross Barkley from Everton, and Nathaniel Chalobah from Chelsea – all guys he had played against in the past.

Harry started on the bench and was called in at the 63rd minute. The game ended in a 1-1 draw. He came on as a 70th-minute substitute in an impressive 3-0 win against Ukraine at the Estadio Algarve on Sunday and played 90-minutes in the 1-1 draw against hosts Portugal in their final match at the Parque Deportivo de Nora, Ferreiras. Although he didn't score, the managers assured him that his performance secured him a spot in the European Championships.

Unfortunately, he couldn't be bothered with a flu shot. And he paid for it. He caught the flu and had to miss the tournament and, with a broken heart, watch his team win it on TV without him.

Back at the Spurs academy, he was part of the Premier League Elite Player Performance. But as usual, he was taken by surprise at how things played out for him. Tim Sherwood was there to greet him when he came back. "I have some good news, Harry," he said as they walked to the fields. "You really have impressed us," he said. "In fact, you've impressed us so much, I'm going to send you away."

Harry stopped in his tracks. "What?"

"We're going to send you out for a few loan spells. We do it because we want you back. In fact, we do it for the select few in our program we know will make it to the first team."

"Thanks," Harry said. "I think." He looked at his coach, unsure of what was about to befall him. "So, what you're really saying is, I'm so good, you're getting rid of me."

Tim laughed. "At least, for a while. It's how we do things around here at this level. It's part of our plan for you. What do you think?"

"Well, sir, *my* plan is to never give up and I think you already know I'll do anything to play for the first team. I'm just not one-hundred percent sure."

Tim smiled and stuck out his hand. "Trust me. I'll get you there."

Harry locked eyes with him and shook his hand.

The next day, he was off on a series of loan spells that would last three years.

In his mind, he saw himself as the Loan Ranger.

CHAPTER 14
GROWING PAINS

Harry felt like a yo-yo. Growing up unnerved him just as much as the yo-yoing he did back and forth from one team to another, going out on loan over the next three years. Somewhere among all that, he started shaving.

He trusted Tim Sherwood, but the initial explanation of the upcoming loan spells, he had to admit, did not sound like fun. Leyton Orient was first. *The O's of League One.* There were very good communications between the Spurs and Leyton. The training grounds of both clubs were so close to each other that the coaches were able to have constant feedback going back and forth about Harry's progress. Still, Harry had to accommodate stepping down, and this was a test of his character. He had to work with fewer staff and more basic facilities. He was sent out on loan spells to get better at the game because they believed in him. But he wasn't sure how this would play out. Still, he was eager to do his best.

Assistant coach Kevin Nugent spoke to Harry about adapting to a new environment. "Look," he said. "If you go out on loan to a club like ours you have to try and learn from every situation."

"I will," Harry said.

"It's about your attitude," Nugent continued. "You have to embrace that sometimes it's not going to be perfect and you are not going to be in your comfort zone. But it helps that you are close to home. You can sleep in your bed every night. It would be much tougher playing in say, Scotland, away from home."

Harry nodded. After his training with Leyton, he could go for additional work with the Spurs. He was still lacking in speed and power. He had a lot of work to do.

That Christmas, he got another card and letter and photo from Katie. She was beautiful. She had written her phone number on the back. Harry stared at it for an hour, then put it in its place of honor in his kit bag.

It took him almost two weeks to work up the nerve to call her, but in January of 2011, just before his debut with Leyton Orient, he called and they talked for two hours. Her voice was just as musical as it was the day he heard her talking with her friends at Chingford, all those years ago.

The day Harry debuted at Rochdale's Spotland Stadium for League One, there was a torrential rainfall. Although it was only raining lightly, a few dozen miles south at Tottenham's Brisbane Road fields, it was pouring at Rochdale. The grounds were waterlogged and Leyton's center forward, Scott McGleish, was exhausted.

"I shouldn't have let this start," Russell Slade, Layton's manager said.

"Too late now," Nugent said.

The teams were tied 1-1 and the game went nowhere. The boys were cold and wet and covered in mud. It was the coldest day of the month. The temperature dropped even further in the late afternoon. There was still seventeen minutes to go. Slade had to bring McGleish off. He looked like a drowned rat, covered in mud. He needed a dry body out there, to give something to the 2,300 diehard fans who had come to support their team.

He glanced over at the bench in the mercifully covered dugout, safe from the rain, and saw 17-year-old Harry Kane.

Harry felt the coach's eyes on him and looked over at him. This was it. He was ready. He wanted to go in.

It happened in a heartbeat. He got the ball to his feet and he charged downfield, his shoes squishing, filled with mud, sloshing up to his ankles, but he maintained control. He served it across to the forward, who missed. But his pass was accurate. And he hadn't made things worse. He looked up in the stands and saw his folks and Charlie, sitting shivering under a couple umbrellas. Charlie stuck out his hand and gave him a thumb's up. It was Charlie's voice in his head that always repeated: *Whatever you do, Harry, don't make things worse.*

He'd got what he wanted. A chance to show his skills, and he never stopped running until the referee ended the game.

Slade and Nugent watched Harry intently. They liked the kid's work ethic.

That night, it took Harry an hour to wash the mud off.

He felt he couldn't just drag now, so most days, after training sessions at Leyton, he would go home to Tottenham and join their practices.

"I'm starting to get the feeling Mr. Sherwood was right about sending me out here," he told Kevin Nugent.

"Of course he was right, but that's none of your business," the O's assistant manager replied. "Your business is to learn from every situation. *That's* why you're here. That includes dealing with disappointments. You're lucky, you get to go home to a warm bed. *Your* bed. Now get back out there and get better, that's what it's all about. Time and experience."

A week later, on a Wednesday, Harry scored his first goal against Sheffield from a free kick from Dean Cox in the 57th minute. Orient won

4-0. He ended his loan spell with Orient scoring five goals in 5 months. It was the second half of the 2010–11 season. He had nine starts and he came in nine more times from the bench. Harry's teammate, McGleish, liked Harry's attitude. Harry never expected to play every game, and he fought with his performances to be picked to play in every game.

Then it was back to the Spurs. At last he was playing with the first team and he even scored one goal in the early stages of a Europa League game. Five games before he was asked to pack his bag again.

Tim Sherwood was waiting for him when he left the changing room. "Let's talk," he said. "How was your loan spell?"

"Tough," Harry said. "But worthwhile."

"They say you have great attitude," Sherwood said. "That you came in and decided you needed to work. You needed to do this to get to your place. And you did just that."

Harry blushed.

"I have no doubt you'll have the same attitude going forward," Sherwood said.

Harry grinned. "Don't tell me," he said. "I'm going again. Like a yo-yo."

Sherwood gave him one of his best smiles. "I gave my word to Kenny Jackett that he could have you. I know you won't let me down."

Kenny Jackett was the manager of Millwall.

Harry stuck out his hand and shook Sherwood's hand. "You don't have to say it; I already know what you're going to say. *Trust me.*"

Sherwood laughed.

Harry and his teammate Ryan Mason joined Millwall and had a slow start. But as the season progressed, he showed his worth and was awarded their Young Player of the Year.

We killed it at Millwall, Harry thought at the end of the season as he slung his kit over his shoulder. He was going home again. To the Spurs.

Joe Gallen was waiting for him. "I have to be honest with you, H. I tried to keep you here," the assistant manager said. "Do you blame me? Five wins in a row? And what a way to finish! You kept us from relegation. What was it? Six in 14 matches?"

"Seven," Harry said.

"Right," Gallen said. "Seven. For a slow start, you blew us all away. It really clicked for you here."

"It was a major battle, Mr. Gallen!" Harry said. "A lot of pressure. It made a man out of me. Plus, my beard came in."

Gallen laughed. "Can I tell you something?"

"Sure," Harry replied.

"In my 20 years of coaching, I've never seen a player practice as hard as you," Gallen said.

"Thank you, sir, that's my thing," Harry replied.

"Every day I had to chuck you off the pitch!"

Harry knew they would love to have had him stay there a lot longer, but he was anxious to go back home; back to White Hart Lane.

The Spurs had other plans.

Pack your bags, Harry!

His next stop was Norwich and it was there, playing against the Donny Rovers from South Yorkshire, where he broke his metatarsal bone.

Harry hated it. Not going back to the Spurs to play. Going back to rehab. He was finally released by the doctor at the end of December of 2012 and returned to Norwich.

He got another card from Katie. And a letter. And a photo. And a new phone number. She was just finishing college and this time, he wasn't going to waste it. He called her the same night he got the letter.

The next day, they started dating.

It was soon after that, that the Spurs came up short a striker and recalled him four months early into the season. But they didn't keep him for long. After 20 days, they sent him down a division to the Foxes at Leicester City.

Harry the yo-yo in a number 37 shirt.

He was there to help the Foxes fight to get into the Premier League when they faced Harry's old team, Watford, at the championship semifinals. Under overcast skies. Their hope of reaching the finals was a mere 90 minutes away.

Harry sat next to Jamie Varney and Danny Drinkwater on the bench. He had played a few weeks earlier and scored one against Blackburn, after which Jamie replaced him off the bench.

As Leicester went down by two, Harry came off the bench. The Foxes came back with a David Nugent header, and with an opportunity to equalize the score, French winger Anthony Knockaert was awarded a penalty in injury time. An equalizer would lift the Foxes to the playoffs final.

The crowd was on their feet.

Harry scanned the crowd and found Katie down front, cheering loudly.

The tension was high. Knockaert took the shot...and keeper Manuel Almunia saved.

Twenty seconds later, in a sweeping counter-attack at the other end, Deeney thumped in a shot and scored just before the whistle.

Harry and his teammates were devastated.

The only ray of light was that his loan ranger days were over. He was back home. And with Katie.

CHAPTER 15
THE SEASON OF DREAMS

Jermain Defoe, who some years ago stopped his Range Rover and played a game of street ball with Harry and his mates, was leaving the Spurs for Major League Soccer in Canada. Harry found Defoe unpacking his locker and stuffing everything into a duffel bag. "Hey," he said.

Jermain looked up. He was holding his number 18 jersey.

"Hey, H, welcome home," he said,

"I just wanted to wish you luck in Toronto with the MLS," Harry said. "What are we going to do for goals?" he continued.

Jermain laughed. *"You'll score them,* that's what." He thought for a moment, then handed him his number 18 jersey. "First Klinsmann, then me, then you? Yeah. You take it. If I'm going to give it to anyone, it should be you. But on one condition."

"What's that?" Harry asked.

"Next time we meet for a pick-up game...be nice."

Harry grinned. "Can't make any promises."

Jermain laughed again and hugged his younger protégé. "I'm gonna miss you, mate. I'm also looking forward to scoring against you. Next time, I won't be so nice either."

Harry smiled. "Yeah, you will," Harry said. Jermain took one last look at the kid he came across on that Chingford street all those years ago, the kid who wanted nothing more than to be a Spur, the kid who became a friend on the team. He zipped up his duffel bag, shouldered it, and left.

During practice, the day before Harry's Premier League debut for Tottenham, Tim Sherwood watched Harry from the touchline. He kicked the first ten exactly where he wanted it but goalkeeper Hugo Lloris did not let them pass. Harry tried again. Lloris had his number. Harry kicked the grass.

That was Sherwood's cue. He marched over to where Harry was running his drills for a chat. "We need to talk," he said.

Harry chuckled. "What'd I do this time? Besides miss every shot?"

"Don't be so hard on yourself, Harry," Sherwood said. "And then put every shot into the bottom corner." He gave Harry a wink, then trotted off the field and stood once more by the touchline, arms crossed, watching intently.

Harry decided to give it a try. He nailed the bottom corner and the ball rolled into the net. He turned and flashed a smile to his coach and Sherwood gave him the thumbs up.

Lloris returned the ball to Harry. "Nice one!"

Harry liked Tim Sherwood a lot. He liked the fact that even when the chips were down, Sherwood was always experimenting. But there was talk of replacing him in the summer.

After the practice game, they had a chat. "If I had to do it over again," Sherwood said, "I wouldn't have let you go out. They hardly played you. I would have kept you from all those loan spells."

"Well, I'm back now. And look at me," Harry said. "Me and the bench are one. *You* may regret it, but *I* don't. I'm grateful you sent me." He thought it was funny, Sherwood sending him off and he not wanting to go and now that he was back home at Tottenham and the man who sent him – wished he hadn't. He had a lot of time to think during those loan spells. Three seasons was a long time.

"Do you remember what you said to me?" Sherwood asked.

Harry thought about. "No," he said.

"You said, 'I've always seen every game I've played as a chance to get to where I want to go'."

Harry smiled. "Yeah, I meant the first team. You sent me anyway."

They laughed.

Harry marched with the Tottenham Hotspur squad out on the field of White Hart Lane on April 7, 2014. He made his Premier start on the bench. Just like he did so many times before on his loan spells; but it was *his* team, *his* home, and it felt amazing. He looked up at Tim Sherwood, who was nearby. "Just like Norwich and Leicester City, and all the rest," Harry quipped and Sherwood smiled.

The crowd roared. He was sure he felt the love. He knew Katie and his folks and Charlie were out there somewhere. His heart beat like a hammer and he was already sweating even though it was a cool day. He felt every step of the perfectly-manicured pitch under his feet.

Sunderland was way down on the totem pole, but as with all things soccer, Harry knew, anything could happen and usually did. In the 17th, Sunderland's Lee Cattermole scored first.

Harry groaned from the bench. He wanted to get out there more than anything. He got his wish at half-time.

Thirteen minutes later, in the 59th, he went to his happy place on the field – down near the goal – and his timing was just right. Christian Eriksen sent a perfectly-aimed cross to him just as he hit the six-yard-box. Harry pivoted and made a late run past the center-back and steered his shot into the bottom corner, completely fooling goalkeeper Vito Mannone, and scored his first Premier League goal.

It worked! he thought. *Just like Tim Sherwood said it would.*

The Spurs won the match 5-1 and on his way off the field, Sherwood pulled alongside Harry. "Get ready for Saturday, Harry," Sherwood said. "You're going in."

"Say that again?" Harry asked.

Sherwood grin. "You're starting for the Spurs, Harry."

A few minutes later, Katie Goodland found Harry and they held hands as they walked to the lot. On the way, they saw a crowd surrounding someone and moved closer for a look. "That's a lot of fans, who is it?" Harry asked.

Katie laughed. "Look!"

The crowd parted revealing the center of attention: his brother Charlie. He was just finishing up signing a program for a girl. Charlie looked up and his eyes grew wide. Harry recognized that look. It was the look he had on his face every time he got into trouble.

In that instant, Harry realized what Charlie was up to.

Someone in the crowd turned and saw Harry. "Hey, wait a minute. *That's* Harry Kane!" The crowd streamed away from Charlie and surrounded Harry, asking for autographs.

Charlie stepped up next to Harry while his younger brother began signing pictures and programs.

"What are you doing? Pretending to be me, Charlie?" Harry whispered.

"I couldn't help it. They thought I was you, so I played along," Charlie replied.

"How could they think you were me, we don't look alike," Harry said, then took another look at his older brother. "Do we?"

Charlie shrugged. "They thought so. So, I was keeping them warm for you."

The brothers laughed and sounded alike.

When the fans were satisfied with their autographs and selfies, Harry and Katie and Charlie crossed to where Pat and Kim waited for them with the car.

"I'm starting Saturday, Dad," Harry said to his father as he piled in, pulling Katie in behind him.

Pat stood there, amazed and turned to Kim. "Starting for the Spurs, he says. Just like that." They chuckled and got in.

And start he did. In fact, Harry had 6 more starts in April and scored in 3 matches in a row.

In May, Tim Sherwood was fired and replaced with Mauricio Pochettino, formerly of Southampton.

Harry watched Pochettino for a full minute before he came out on the field. He felt his short scratchy beard. It relaxed him to know there was at least one thing in this day that was inevitable. He had checked himself out in the mirror just minutes before. He liked the way he looked. He was, however, worried sick about something.

Pochettino studied his clipboard and scribbled some notes.

Harry trotted to the new coach but instead of continuing on to the field, he stopped. "Mr. Pochettino?"

Pochettino looked up from his clipboard. "Yes, Harry?"

"I heard you signed a new goalkeeper."

"Yes, I'm very happy with him."

"And some defenders."

Pochettino wondered what was eating his prodigy. "Yes. And a midfielder too," he said. "All good men." Then he stopped looking at the clipboard and turned his gaze on Harry, who shifted uncomfortably from one foot to the other.

"You know; we have very nice toilets in the clubhouse. Always go before you come out on the field, makes life a whole lot easier," Pochettino said with a smile.

"Oh! No, sir!" Harry stammered, mortified, and laughed nervously. "I-I don't have to go."

"All right, then what's bothering you?"

"I was just wondering if maybe you had also signed a new center forward?"

Pochettino smiled. *So that was it.* "No, Harry, I did not sign a new center forward. I already have Emmanuel, Roberto, and most importantly, I have *you*. Everything is good. And by the way, since you brought it up – you're doing great. It's going to be a big season for you."

Harry brightened immediately. "Yes, sir!" He loped off.

Pochettino watched, amused, then returned his attention to his clipboard. He understood why Harry was worried. He was worried as well. His own start as a manager was less than stellar. In his first nine league matches, they had lost to Liverpool, West Brom, Manchester City, and Newcastle. The chairman of Tottenham, Daniel Levy, was impulsive when it came to making changes. He thought he might go the way of Tim Sherwood. His friend Frank de Boer had already been given his walking papers by Crystal Palace after just four matches. It seemed to be contagious throughout the league.

Pochettino knew his job was on the line by November and his upcoming match as manager was against Aston Villa.

On game day at the Lane, Pochettino knew he had a not-so-secret weapon in *Harry Kane the Hurricane*.

Harry first heard it from the parking lot. The fans already in the stadium were singing the song of praise.

HE'S ONE OF OUR OWN,

HE'S ONE OF OUR OWN,

SOMETHING SOMETHING – HE'S ONE OF OUR OWN!

He couldn't quite make out the name. Nacer Chadli, walked alongside him with a broad smile. Harry looked at him. "That's for you, mate," Harry said and slapped Chadli's back. "Congratulations."

Chadli laughed. "You must be deaf, H!" he said as he and Harry and the rest of the team approached the entrance. "That chant is for you! You've arrived, mate! You're finally a Spur!"

Harry felt his heart race with excitement. It was that thing that happens when your dreams come true. That magic.

The singing was much clearer as they approached and Harry finally heard for himself that they were singing for him.

HE'S ONE OF OUR OWN,
HE'S ONE OF OUR OWN,
HARRY KANE – HE'S ONE OF OUR OWN!

Harry's eyes grew wet and he wiped his tears on his sleeve. He knew the song because he remembered it from all the Spurs matches he attended with Mom and Dad and Charlie at the Lane, growing up. It was a song sung to the players who they felt belonged to them, men like Jermain Defoe and Teddy Sheringham. And now they were singing for him. Harry Kane.

They went in and prepared for the match.

Harry was not starting, despite him having scored eight times that season, all of them in cup competitions.

Pochettino was holding the Hurricane back.

The singing continued at the 16th when Villa's Charles N'Zogbia avoided Danny Rose and crossed to Andreas Weimann, who stuffed it into the net. Aston Villa's drought was over and the Spurs were down 1-0.

The fans chanted non-stop for Harry.

In fact, the singing seemed to last forever.

At the half, Pochettino raised the stakes and the tension by keeping Harry on the bench at the half and replacing Christian Eriksen with Erik Lamela instead.

The fans responded in kind:

WE WANT OUR TOTTENHAM BACK!

At the 65th, Villa's Christian Benteke went too far with his rough-housing and pushed Ryan Mason in the face; he was sent off with a red card and at the 84th, Nacer Chadli took advantage and swept in to equalize the score.

Tick-tock.

The fans never gave up and chanted for Harry Kane the Hurricane.

Pochettino checked his watch. At the 90th, he appeased the wild fans and called in Harry and gave them what they wanted. The crowd went nuts.

Moments later, Carlos Sanchez tripped Andros Townsend just outside the goal area and Harry stepped in for the free-kick.

Harry chipped the ball 20-yards, deflected off defender Nathan Baker, and the ball sailed smoothly into the net.

The Tottenham fans erupted in a roar that rattled windows. Harry jubilantly raced ahead of his mates to the Spurs side and slid on his stomach on the wet grass, surrounded by his mates. The cheering went on for minutes.

Harry had saved the day. And Mauricio Pochettino got to keep his job.

Harry went on and scored another 100 goals for Tottenham, many of them against teams who had left him on the bench. He played on 5 national teams and made his senior debut for England at Wembley on March 27, 2015. He became the all-time Tottenham scorer, beating his hero Teddy Sheringham's scoring record by one, and tying Cristiano Ronaldo and Leo Messi's record of scoring 13 goals in a single month.

In January 2017, Katie and Harry had their first child, a daughter, Ivy, and in July, on a vacation in the Bahamas, Harry got down on one knee on the beach, and proposed to his childhood sweetheart.

And at age 24, in 2017, Harry won 75% of the England Supporters Club's votes, having scored braces against France and Malta and scored in fixtures with Scotland, Slovenia, and Lithuania, and was voted the 2017 Vauxhall England Men's Player of the Year.

2018 was an even better year. With a second baby on the way, another daughter, Three Lions coach Gareth Southgate handed Harry the captain's armband, and together with the youngest English squad in UK history, went to the World Cup in Russia.

CHAPTER 16
THE GOLDEN BOY

England played brilliantly in the group stage of the World Cup and Harry, wearing the captain's armband, led his team to the semi-finals – doing what they had managed only to do 28 years before, in Italy.

Harry scored six goals in previous matches against Tunisia, Panama, and Columbia, but he was scoreless in his semi-final match against Croatia, and England lost 1-2.

The Three Lions went home.

Katie and Harry watched the final together.

"All six of your shots were on target," said Katie.

"I needed a few more," replied Harry.

"You did great." Katie smiled.

"I don't know," Harry replied with uncertainty.

"The team did more than getting to the semi-finals. You brought all of us together."

Harry smiled at Katie, the girl who always knew the right thing to say. She was right this time too. The team had reconnected with the fans, and helped bring the whole country together. Only when the team was back did he realize what it was like back home. When he was in Russia, Harry and the team were in their bubble and didn't understand what was going on until they saw the videos of the reaction of the English people.

Everyone said how amazing it was, and that's the most important thing, Harry thought. Bringing pride back to the fans. Bringing back hope that the team can do even better down the road.

France beat Croatia 4-2 and took home the World Cup. Harry and Katie watched as it was announced he had won the Golden Boot for top scorer.

The only other Englishman to get it since Gary Lineker in 1986.

A week later, the FA handed Harry the Golden Boot statuette. Katie gave it a place of honor in the living room, between the two Premier League Golden Boots.

His phone rang. It was David Beckham.

"Well done, Harry," Becks said. "You're part of soccer history."

Harry remembered how all those years ago he wanted to be just like Beckham. When Becks got a Mohawk haircut, he did the same thing. He was the laughing stock of his friends until it grew out. He thought about how his dreams had come true many times over. He couldn't have done it without his mom and dad and Charlie;

without the great coaches and role models like Defoe and Sheringham and Beckham. And he couldn't have done it without sheer dedication, hard work, and perseverance.

"Thank you," he said.

THE WORLD'S #1 BEST-SELLING SOCCER SERIES!

THE FLEA

The Amazing Story of Leo Messi

Michael Part

Cristiano Ronaldo
The Rise of a Winner

Michael Part

Neymar
The Wizard

Michael Part

Luis Suarez
A Striker's Story

Michael Part

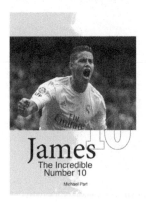

James
The Incredible
Number 10

Michael Part

Balotelli
The Untold
Story

Michael Part

Learn more at www.solebooks.com